T0036155

TO:

FROM:

Praise for **THE GENIUS HABIT**

"Give yourself the gift of genius—not through inborn luck but through Laura Garnett's powerful, practical system to build a lifelong Genius Habit. Bored at work? Instead of berating yourself, consider that your plateaus are signals pointing toward greater purpose. This book will help you dismantle barriers to find what really lights you up as you click into the contagious joy of doing the work you—and only you—were born to do."

—**JENNY BLAKE**, author of *Pivot: The Only Move That Matters Is Your Next One*

"Work doesn't have to feel like, well, work. With Laura's advice, you can find your Zone of Genius, accomplish more, and stop counting the minutes until quitting time."

—**LAURA VANDERKAM**, author of *Off the Clock: Feel Less Busy While Getting More Done*

"Laura Garnett has written a powerful guide to finding and sustaining success and joy in your work. She has helped me and many other people get in touch with our essence and our unique gifts and coached us on how to live and work in that zone for an ever-growing proportion of our lives. The results are nothing short of astounding on all fronts. Life can hold so much more satisfaction and delight than we can imagine, and this book shows us how to unlock that."

—**RAJ SISODIA**, cofounder and chairman emeritus of Conscious Capitalism International

"There is a genius hiding in all of us, and if you haven't found yours, you are probably dreading every Monday morning drive to work. Most of us go a lifetime searching for joy at work. Finding your genius is the key. It turns out there is a genius habit you can develop, and Laura Garnett shows us how. In following her timeless advice, we can get to the joy we always dreamed was possible and become the person we were destined to be."

—**RICH SHERIDAN,** author of *Joy, Inc.* and *Chief Joy Officer*

FIND YOUR
ZONE
of
GENIUS

How to

→ REDEFINE INTELLIGENCE

→ BECOME AN EXPERT ON YOURSELF

→ AND MAKE GREATNESS A GIVEN

LAURA GARNETT

Internal images © end sheets, suksunt sansawast/Getty Images; page viii, 106,
twomeows/Getty Images; page xiv, Peter Dazeley/Getty Images; page xx, Luis
Alvarez/Getty Images; page 2, 12, 23, Westend61/Getty Images; page 7, 100, Klaus
Vedfelt/Getty Images; page 16, alphaspirit/Getty Images; page 28, suedhang/Getty
Images; page 35, ExperienceInteriors/Getty Images; page 40, FlamingoImages/Getty
Images; page 50, Sunwoo Jung/Getty Images; page 57, ljubaphoto/Getty Images;
page 62, Ekspansio/Getty Images; page 69, susan.k./Getty Images; page 74, Hill
Street Studios/Getty Images; page 81, anyaberkut/Getty Images; page 84, Orbon
Alija/Getty Images; page 91, Andrew Bret Wallis/Getty Images; page 96, Astrakan
Images/Getty Images; page 103, Rob Lewine/Getty Images
Internal image on page 110 was provided Unsplash; this image is licensed under CC0
Creative Commons and was released by the author for use.

Published by Simple Truths, an imprint of Sourcebooks
P.O. Box 4410, Naperville, Illinois 60567-4410
(630) 961-3900
sourcebooks.com

Printed and bound in China.
OGP 10 9 8 7 6 5 4 3 2 1

FOR ZOE,
thank you for giving me the
gift of witnessing you cultivate
your own Zone of Genius

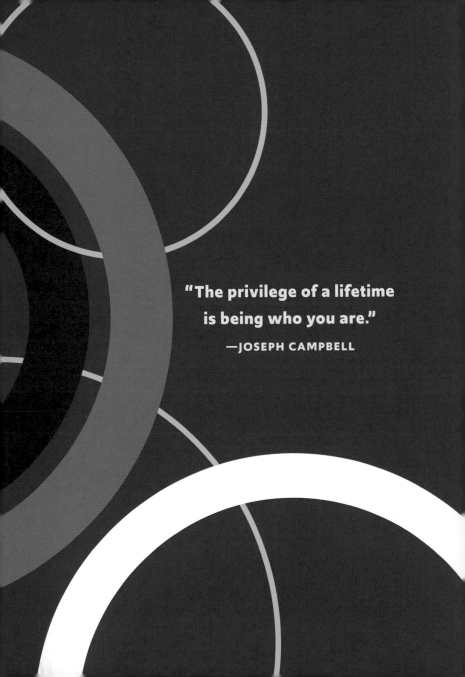

"The privilege of a lifetime
is being who you are."

—JOSEPH CAMPBELL

CONTENTS

→ INTRODUCTION

I was watching yet another documentary about a super successful person (my favorite genre). This time, it was about Bill Gates, in the documentary called *Inside Bill's Brain*. During the interview, Bill talked about how he knew as a kid that he had the ability to rapidly digest lots of information and synthesize it to come up with ways to solve really complex problems. The more complex, the more energized he seemed to be. He started doing this when he was eight. He was solving complex problems for schools and for other companies.

I watch documentaries like this all the time, and this was probably one of the most obvious examples of someone knowing what their genius is—the thinking or problem solving they're best at—valuing it, and then using it all the time. In fact, he described being really obstinate and against rules. He fought regularly with his mother, and as he matured, he opted out of environments that prevented him from working in the way he wanted to, such as college. This way of operating is usually not considered good behavior, nor would it ever be suggested as the right path to success. Yet Bill is a multibillionaire; by our society's measuring system, he's one of the most successful men in the United States. Following society's direction was clearly not the right path for Bill, and it's often not the right path for anyone who creates success that is aligned with who they really are. But what was more apparent to me in listening to him was that he's also successful in other ways most of us crave. He's continually challenged by his work, so much so that he would do it for free. He also seems to be intrinsically motivated by the impact he is creating. Solving some of the world's most notable problems, such as eradicating polio worldwide, creating a way to cut carbon emissions by 50 percent, and providing clean water for those who don't have it, are clearly linked to a rewarding feeling that he's helping people who can't help themselves. There is no doubt in my mind that Bill is fully operating in his Zone of Genius every day.

What I observed in the documentary was that Bill wasn't motivated by money or power; he was just doing the kind of thinking and problem solving that he wants to do *every day* while having an impact that is meaningful to him. This is what creates real success. You have to wake up wanting to do the work that you do because it's fun, exciting, and rewarding, not because of the accolades, pay, or power.

It took me thirty-five years before I learned what it was like to have work that I loved in the same way I see in Bill. In fact, I don't just love my job; my work is an extension of who I am, and it pushes me to be who I want to be. It is my constant source of energy. When

I was experiencing overwhelming sickness during my first trimester of pregnancy, my work gave me strength to carry on. I don't daydream about what I could be doing with my career or life because I'm already doing it. I never thought it would be possible to feel this way about my job, but I do.

While what I just described may sound idyllic, it did not come easily. Creating a job I'm intellectually challenged by and emotionally attached to required a lot of work. I've always been ambitious, but I had no clue what I wanted to do with my life after college. Throughout my childhood, I was taught that the path to success was paved with good grades, college, and a job—any well-paying job. My parents rarely talked about prioritizing happiness or job satisfaction. What really mattered was *financial security*.

Even though I knew the rules I was supposed to follow, my path was a bit different. I spent two years after college exploring: I waited tables, moved to Holland to be an au pair, then came back home and started a master's degree in nutrition before deciding it wasn't a good fit after all. I hopped into other roles, eventually landing in the wine industry as an executive assistant to the CEO. The work wasn't very exciting or challenging, but I thought it was a stepping-stone to something that was: wine sales. However, the company downsized and decided to eliminate my job. Fortunately, a friend who was working for Capital One told me they were hiring and expanding rapidly. I took a chance and applied.

I was hired as a marketing manager. They offered me a salary I previously couldn't even have imagined, exponentially higher than anything I had earned before. I remember jumping up and down, screaming with joy and feeling like my life had just started. Capital One's philosophy was that you could learn on the job, which was great because I'd never done marketing before. Once I got there, I ramped up my efforts to succeed at the job, and I learned as I went. Eventually, I applied to join the marketing and analysis group, which at Capital

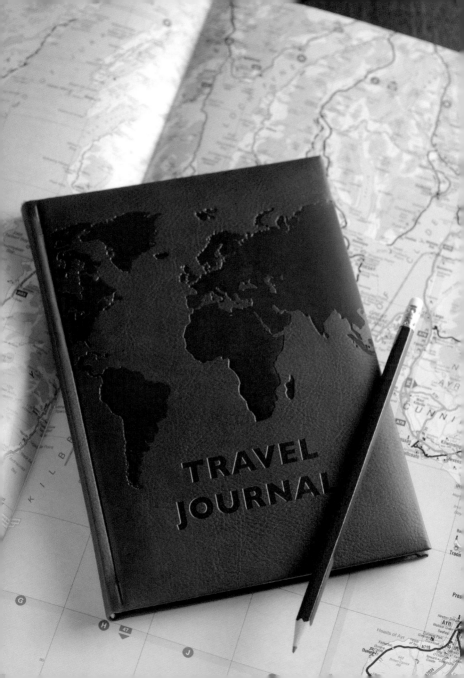

One was the crème de la crème. I decided I needed to be in this top-notch department because it would look good on my résumé. It would also make me feel important and smart—something I yearned to feel.

I was hired into the department and moved to Washington, DC. Within three weeks of my arrival, the management team decided to dissolve my group. But this was in the heyday of Capital One, so the restructuring was actually an amazing opportunity. If anything, it was a huge door opener, because my manager asked me, "What do you want to do next?"

I had the travel bug, so I answered, "What are we doing internationally? How can I get on an international team?" There was one small group in South Africa that was hiring, and two weeks later, I got on a plane. I lived in South Africa for two years. The group was highly entrepreneurial in the sense that we were building a business from scratch. Every day, I was tackling the jobs of twenty-five people back in the United States. It was a huge confidence builder for me, because I was thriving, I was excited, and I was adding value. On top of that, I met a guy, fell in love, and got married. He was also working for Capital One and living in South Africa for a short stint.

From there, we were both sent to Spain, London, and finally Washington, DC, and that's where the Capital One party ended. Once we were back in the United States, I felt more like I was working for a large organization, which was completely different from the international start-ups. It didn't take long in my new role to realize I wasn't having fun anymore. I was uninspired by the tasks and projects I was managing. I didn't see how what I did made any real difference or impact on the business. I had a job that was largely operational, not strategic, and I lost all energy and enthusiasm for going to work. I was bored and uninspired, and even more upsetting, I didn't see a role that I wanted to move into. My husband felt similarly, and we decided to move on. We packed our bags and moved to New York.

Within a month, I ended up at Google in a sales job, and I was ecstatic—at first. In 2005, Google was the company to work for, and it immediately gave me bragging rights. Yet to my dismay, the moment I got there, I knew it was a terrible fit. I lacked autonomy—I had to respond immediately to clients' needs, which seemed never-ending, and I had little control over my day-to-day work.

For the first time in my life, I experienced something that I had only heard about from others: I dreaded going to work. It was a hard time for me—I hated my job, and my marriage was beginning to crumble.

Rather than look for another job, I decided to stick it out and stay in my role for a year, knowing that I could then switch departments. After the first year, I applied to another position that seemed like a better fit, and for the first ten months, it was. I also got divorced and was doing the work to move on with my life. I was excited about work again, but my happiness was short-lived. My department went through a reorganization, and my job changed, putting me back in a role that wasn't right for me.

Even though I knew I was in the wrong job, I was addicted to the benefits: free food, free drinks, free snacks, and five-dollar massages (I think I got one every other day). My manager started talking to me about my "inability to succeed" in my role. I knew this job was not something I was good at, but I just couldn't stomach the idea of failure. I was put on a performance plan, which was crushing. I started thinking, *I'm thirty-three. What is the work that I'm really meant to do? Why haven't I figured this out yet?*

One day at the Google office, I went to hear bestselling author Srikumar Rao speak. He asked the crowd, "Can you imagine waking up every morning and getting on your hands and knees and being so grateful for the job and life that you have that you're almost in tears of joy every morning?" I wanted that feeling, and I knew I didn't have it, even though to the outside world, it looked like everything in my life was going fine.

But it wasn't. I questioned everything. *What am I best at? What am I meant to do? How can I create the kind of career and success I dream about?* I read every book I could find on careers and success and struggled to find concrete answers. I started an exhaustive job search, found a job quickly at a start-up, and quit Google. The start-up didn't last. I was there for nine months, but within a month, I knew that I was in another job that wasn't a great fit. I felt frustrated and as though I would never be able to find work that was right for me. I questioned my future, my value, and myself. Then, I got laid off. I will never forget that day—I was escorted out of the Frank Gehry building on the west side of Manhattan, and in that moment, I decided that if my dream job doesn't exist, I was going to create it from scratch.

Miraculously, I got a call from Srikumar Rao, whom I had seen speak several times since his talk at Google. I had approached him after one of those talks and said that I was interested in working for him. Now he was calling to take me up on that offer, and I was ecstatic!

In my role as his head of sales and operations, I helped him grow his business of helping people get happy. Throughout my time working with him, I watched and learned. He taught me the valuable lesson that **happiness is not just something bestowed upon lucky people**. Instead, happiness comes with daily practice; it is a habit you can cultivate. When I realized that my happiness was up to me, I worked every day on owning my power and my confidence, and soon after, happiness began to come. Developing this habit of creating my own happiness was an essential building block in creating the work that I do now.

After working with Srikumar Rao as well as Esther Perel, another bestselling author in the personal growth field, I was ready for a complete pivot. I realized that working with them wasn't really my calling. I knew I wanted to work with entrepreneurs but on my own terms. I found that the part of my business I enjoyed most was brand building. I realized that to build a successful brand, you have to know who you are. And when I dug deeper, I realized it wasn't the actual branding that excited me; it was discovering who my clients were and how they could use this information to enhance their overall careers, not just grow their small businesses. Once I realized it was careers that I wanted to focus on, I pivoted again. I went back to my corporate roots and targeted leaders in the corporate world.

My business grew through lots of trial and error, and along the way I realized that the moments when

I enjoyed my work the most, when I was in the *zone*, occurred when I was asking people questions and seeing patterns in their responses that turned into insights and ultimately actionable steps they could use to create positive change. **This was the work and the thinking that really lit me up.** Whenever I did it, I completely lost track of time and felt as though I was on fire. Over time, I found I could easily create more of these moments each day where I could use my unique way of problem solving. The more I practiced it, the stronger it became and the more excited I felt about my work.

Today, I consider myself to be a successful performance strategist. I have become an expert in helping people understand the specific behaviors and habits required to perform at a very high level in their chosen careers. I've synthesized all the latest research and distilled the groundbreaking thinking from across industries into a process that allows people to incorporate these lessons into their lives. By using these tools, my clients learn that the key to achieving their best life and a job they love is to really understand who they are and what they are best at, and then to take this knowledge and implement it in their work every day. By doing so, *anyone* can take more ownership of their career.

Is Happiness at Work Even Possible?

You may have experienced all the things I've gone through in my working life. You may feel unsatisfied with your job. You may feel unfulfilled. You may be trying to be someone you're not. My goal is to help you glean a better understanding of who you really are so that you can use your most powerful asset at work: you.

I promise that you don't need to think like Albert Einstein to find and develop your genius. Genius is in each and every one of us. All you have to do is identify it within yourself and learn how to best apply it to your work every day. I hope the information in this book will help you gain clarity about who you are and where you're going so you can proactively create the career of your dreams.

PART 1

Challenge

chapter 1

Why Is It So Hard to Be Yourself at Work?

You are born being exactly who you are. Spend time with a toddler and you will see that while they have little awareness of what others think, they are purely authentic. This starts to curb once kids get messages about what is right, what is expected, what is good, and what is bad. As those messages are shared, an internal shift starts to happen, and it can often be a first shift away from the authentic self they were born to be. This shift can continue and usually does in dramatic ways, so that by the time you are a young adult, you can be completely detached from who you are.

There is also no formal education provided on being yourself or fully embodying your true potential. I hope this changes by the time my three-year-old daughter is in high school. Learning how to filter outside messages that can steer you in directions that are in opposition to yourself, discard them, or process them from a place of confidence is a skill that is badly needed for leading happy and authentic lives. It's also essential for making your life a process of becoming who you are. If we could learn how to be who we are before we become adults rather than much later, navigating life and career decisions would not be the struggle that they often are.

Not Succeeding Is Often a Job-Fit Problem

What's more, many people hold fast to antiquated ideas about work in general. *If you can't stay focused at work, it's because there's something wrong with you. If you find a particular task difficult, it's because you're incompetent or lazy.* Some people become so demoralized that they give up on a company or industry long before they have had a chance to diagnose the real problem, and they will likely find themselves back in the same situation in a few years. Others start working long hours to overcompensate for what they perceive to be a lack of skill or competence. This can create even more anxiety about job performance.

This book is meant to help you get more connected to yourself and figure out your Zone of Genius. By identifying your Zone of Genius and adjusting your work so that it revolves around your genius and purpose, you avoid the feelings of confusion and anxiety about work that many people can't escape. Instead of feeling like a victim of circumstance, you will be able to navigate work challenges and career transitions with ease. You will also be able to more easily diagnose job-fit problems or see when being who you are is not possible. You will see that scenario as a problem to solve, not a sign that you're not valuable and you need to be someone or something you're not to succeed. Getting to know yourself and your Zone of Genius is a journey and a critical stepping-stone to success, a stepping-stone that is often never used.

Society Steers You in the Wrong Direction

The other problem with being yourself is that society conspires to keep you from yourself. This sounds strange, but when you take the messages we all get from others and compare them to the science of performance, it's very clear that society is wrong all the time. You are also hard-wired from birth to believe what your parents think is right. Unfortunately, most parents aren't career experts and are thinking more about themselves and what they want for their kids rather than what is actually right for them. It takes a new paradigm of parenting to raise a child to truly be themselves (which I'm currently practicing), and that new paradigm requires more effort than most are

willing to exert. Here are some messages from society that probably sound familiar:

▶ Going to college is imperative for a successful career.

▶ IQ is connected to success.

▶ How you do in school is a sign of your future potential.

▶ Failures are a sign you are a failure.

▶ Benefits and job security are more important than loving the work.

▶ How something looks is more important than how it makes you feel.

▶ Company brand recognition is more important than your happiness.

▶ If you make a lot of money, you will be successful and happy.

▶ When you're more successful than others, you are more valuable.

▶ Follow the advice of other successful people. If it worked for them, it should work for you.

▶ Don't quit until you have another job lined up.

You may not think you're operating from these rules, but when you think through all the decisions you've made in your career, you will be surprised at how much these rules show up. Part of being who you are is ignoring these rules. We accept these messages as truth because our brains are wired to conform to the thinking of the crowd. Psychologist Solomon Asch conducted an experiment in the 1950s that crystallized his research on groupthink. His experiments featured groups of people making basic decisions about whether a set of lines matched in size. He planted actors in the room to purposely give false answers and found that when the majority of people gave a particular answer (even if it was false), the unaware person went along with the group. This connection to conformity and avoidance of conflict is so deeply entrenched in the brain that we react to disagreements in a similar manner to punishment. This is one powerful reason why it is so difficult to go against the groupthink of what work is supposed to look and feel like and stay steadfast in your belief that it should be fun and right for you. It's much easier to follow the lead of those around you, conform, and follow society's rules that often keep you in a job that isn't the right fit but may look like it is to others. This is also why outside-the-box thinking is a rebellious act of stepping out of your comfort zone and why creating a new kind of work, where you are who you are and love what you do, requires being a maverick.

This book is meant to introduce you to a new rule book: you. Who you are should become the new voice of reason, because when you're clear about who you are, decisions come more easily. You don't have to lean on society's erroneous rules.

Using Your Genius Makes Hard Work Energizing

The right kind of work challenges should be hard, but in a good way. These challenges occur when you are thinking, processing, and problem solving a specific task. You know that you're capable of coming up with the right answers; you just haven't figured out all the pieces yet. There's a positive energy about this challenge: you're looking forward to solving the problem and getting the right outcome. What feels exciting and energizing to you is that tension between knowing what you can do and wondering how exactly you will do it.

Mihaly Csikszentmihalyi, the pioneering psychologist and author of the groundbreaking book *Flow*, has his own definition for this kind of challenge: "The best moments usually occur when a person's body or mind is stretched to its limits in a voluntary effort to accomplish something difficult and worthwhile." In other words, you are most engaged when you are doing

11

work that pushes you beyond your comfort zone yet isn't so stressful that it inhibits enjoyment.

Csikszentmihalyi uses this definition to describe *flow*: when you're in flow, you're so immersed in what you're doing that you lose track of time. You feel confident, and the work is invigorating. In fact, Csikszentmihalyi's research found that people are happiest when they're working, as long as the work is something they enjoy and is sufficiently challenging.

Csikszentmihalyi defines challenging work, or flow, as meeting three criteria:

1 **The work must contain a goal that you can measure yourself against.** For me, this refers to the ability to see progression and a specific outcome.

2 **You need to have feedback on that goal.** You should seek out valid confirmation that your goal has been achieved.

3 **You must have a good balance between the perceived challenges of the task and your own perceived skills.** This is what I call the sweet spot of challenge.

When I first read Csikszentmihalyi's definition of flow, what stood out for me was that most people are meeting the first two criteria: they are setting goals and getting feedback on their ability to achieve that goal. But most people don't know how to create the third part of the equation. Without an understanding of yourself (which most people sadly don't have), it's almost impossible to know how to create flow.

What Kind of Success Is Right for You?

Here is one question to think about, and the answer isn't one that can be tracked or quantified. This is the kind of question that might reveal your hidden biases, hopes, and fears about work. So much of knowing yourself better involves letting go of what others have told you about achievement and success and learning to trust that your version of success doesn't have to be the same as that of society, your colleagues, or your family.

What is your definition of success?

When I ask myself this question, success is spending the majority of my time on work or tasks that are fulfilling, leveraging my Zone of Genius, maximizing my potential, and helping other people in a meaningful way while achieving the freedom, lifestyle, and experiences I desire.

The Next Step

Now, let's get started identifying your genius. It's time to start asking the right questions and figuring out how you like to work.

chapter

2

Identifying Your Genius

Are you challenged at work in a way that feels engaging, fun, and, dare I say, exhilarating? If the answer is no, you probably aren't using your genius. Albert Einstein was considered a genius because of his IQ, but if you watch *Genius* on National Geographic, in which the first season tells the story of his life, you quickly see that Einstein's impact went beyond just his IQ. He was told by his teachers that he wouldn't amount to anything because he resisted following the rigidity of the school's thinking. He was ridiculed by the physics community because his thinking was like nothing they had seen and was beyond what they knew. His success and impact in the world were not because he was a genius but because he actively used his genius for a lifetime and worked tirelessly to apply it in infinite ways. Picasso, featured in the second season, didn't have the IQ of a genius, but we think of him as one. There are countless other examples of people refer- ring to someone as a genius when real knowledge of their IQ is not possible. Why is this? It's because when someone is doing the work they are meant to do, they create things that are genius. The reason more people aren't doing work we consider genius has nothing to do with their lack of ability; it's that they haven't been taught the art of using what they're best at and using it often. Einstein and Picasso believed in themselves and didn't question their abilities. They knew they had something unique and special to offer the world. And so do you!

Your genius is the kind of thinking or problem solv- ing that you're best at. When you're using your genius at work, time flies. It's a visceral feeling that many people describe as *being in the zone*—fully engaged and challenged in a way that is not too easy or too hard. You're heavily immersed in your work and not bothered by distractions. You're challenged but not overwhelmed. You're excited, and you feel a sense of confidence and accomplishment. You feel as though you're on fire.

My client Steve finds that he is most challenged when he is having informative conversations with a variety of people, understanding their opinions and ideas, then creating one cohesive strategy that addresses all their needs. The process of collaborating and pulling all the ideas into one concept is his favorite and most effective method of working, so we named his genius *Collaborative Synthesizing Strategist*.

Another client, Chelsea, learned that her genius was as a *Vision Builder*. She was in the zone when she was taking a vision that someone else created and building it. What was fascinating about Chelsea is that a critical part of her using her genius was having the ideal visionary partner. We were also able to get clear on what kind of genius her ideal partner should have in order for her to be able to seek him or her out.

I spend a lot of time talking with my clients about when they are in the zone. I help them pinpoint what the unique thinking is that gets them there, I put a name to it, and I help them notice when they're using it and when they're not. I've also found that once you identify the thinking that is most exciting to you, you can actually home in on it and figure out how to use that type of thinking more often.

This idea of using your genius to attain excellence has been missing in the literature and cultural attitudes about career success, which tend to focus on more basic characteristics that have been universally accepted as positive and effective. Performing well on standardized tests, getting good grades, and being outgoing are traits often considered inherent to success. But when you look at what's critical for long-lasting success, you see that it's driven by being intellectually challenged by the work you're doing. You are so engaged in this thinking, you want to do it all the time. This drive is what's needed to persevere through failures and never give up, two things that science tells us are essential for success.

Genius Action Plan: Identify How You Like to Think at Work Now

The first step to identifying your genius is to find the places in your job where you already use it. Let's pinpoint the moments when you feel in the zone. Ask yourself the following questions. Resist the urge to say the "right" thing or the smart thing, the thing you think your manager wants to hear, or the thing you think will bring you the most recognition and accolades.

1 What are the moments and the tasks I am doing when I am in the zone at work? These are the times where I'm intellectually on fire, stimulated, and energized by the thinking that I'm doing.

2 What is the type of thinking or problem solving that caused this intellectual challenge to occur?

Next, think about three work projects you have completed during which you felt you were really in the zone. Write down every step you took to accomplish each project, from start to finish. Think about how enjoyable each step was and rate it, on a scale from 1 to 10, with 10 being the most enjoyable. Now, focus on the steps that you rated 8 or higher. You should see a pattern that relates specifically to the process that you follow to use your genius. You could be working alone, as part of a team, or both. The various steps that you typically follow to do your genius thinking become your genius process. This process is the repeatable way that you use your genius most easily.

If you can't think of any moments when you were in the zone, you may not be using your genius very often in your current job. This experience is not all that uncommon. It means you've probably been

trying to change yourself to fit the job rather than embrace who you are. Never fear. If that is the case, you have the most opportunity for improving your current experience of work. Instead, see if you can notice when you're most engaged at home or in your personal life. Which tasks are you naturally drawn to? What is the problem solving or thinking that most appeals to you?

For those struggling to see it, here are some additional tips for determining when you are in the zone at work:

▶ Slow down. You may be going through your days so quickly that you don't pay attention to the moments when you feel challenged and engaged.

▶ Start mapping out the moments when you're really bored or even frustrated at work. What is making you feel this way? Pay attention to the thinking or the tasks that you truly hate, and try to turn them on their heads. See if your frustrations can help guide you to the problem solving that you really enjoy. For example, a lot of "big idea" people get frustrated or bored with talking about normal day-to-day business operations.

▶ Create opportunities that will challenge you by putting yourself in situations that seem a bit scary but exciting. These are the bread crumbs that will lead you to your genius. Track what you're feeling when you don't quite have the solution to a problem but it feels like one is just around the corner. Pay attention to the moment when insight finally strikes. What was the thinking that was happening? What kind of problem solving, if any, were you doing? What was the process that you enjoyed that got you to accomplish a task?

After you have tracked the moments when you're in the zone, take the data you've collected and ask yourself the following questions:

▶ What patterns are emerging?

▶ What is the thinking that I am doing that is most enjoyable?

▶ Is there a single type of problem that I am solving?

▶ How do I approach problem solving differently from others around me?

▶ What can I name what I'm seeing?

How Your Personality Informs Your Genius

Your personality is something you were born with. It is how you engage with the world. It evolves over the course of your life and influences your particular genius. The standard identification of personality type is the Myers-Briggs Type Indicator (MBTI). The MBTI is an introspective, self-reported questionnaire that defines how people perceive the world around them and make decisions. The original versions of the MBTI were constructed by two Americans, Katharine

Cook Briggs and her daughter Isabel Briggs Myers. It is based on a theory proposed by noted psychologist Carl Jung, who believed that there are four principal psychological functions by which humans experience the world—sensation, intuition, feeling, and thinking—and that one of these four functions is dominant for each person most of the time. According to Jung, we have specific preferences in the way we take part in these functions, which are critical when working with other people.

Knowing this information is important because it helps you understand what kinds of people and places are your ideal working environments. More often than not, when you experience conflict at work, it's a result of different personality types at play.

Your personality and your genius are two distinctive aspects of who you are, and it's important for your personal and professional selves to understand both of them. Your genius defines the kind of work you will be most successful doing, and your personality will help

you find the right environment for you, including the kind of people and business culture that is the best fit for who you are and how you naturally operate.

Name Your Genius

Language is powerful and it can help communicate your genius more effectively to others. Creating a name for your genius is the best way to not only honor it but also remember it. It's hard to describe ourselves to others, and in the absence of specific language, we default to using general terms that could be applied to almost anyone. Words like smart, motivated, and hard-working all sound great, but what do they actually mean? Are there stronger words you can use? Are there more accurate synonyms to describe your exact strengths? Does the language clearly define your thought process? When I share that my genius is an *Insight Excavator* and explain what that means, it feels clear, descriptive, and personal. It allows someone else to connect easily with the value that I offer.

Now, create a phrase that best describes your genius. Practice using it. Does it feel right? Is it enjoyable to share with others? If it's not, keep playing around with the wording. You know you've hit on the right phrase when it describes you so well that you finally feel as though others can understand you.

Here are some of my favorite genius names and descriptions.

Can you find your genius in any of these suggestions?

Process Creation: Making Everything Work Better

- ▶ **Chaos-to-Order Problem Solver:** You thrive by bringing order to chaotic situations.
- ▶ **Ideal Process Developer:** You can easily create processes that bring order to disorganized situations.
- ▶ **Improvement Strategist:** You constantly look for ways to improve processes, people, and work by streamlining the way things operate.

► **Needle Finder:** You are driven by the process of finding solutions that are extremely hard to find.

► **Process Architect:** You are innately drawn to figuring out the clear steps needed to make things happen in an organized and efficient manner.

► **Good-to-Great Strategist:** You are challenged by taking an existing process or business from good to great.

Visionary: Redefining the World

► **Barrier-Breaking Visionary:** You are challenged when you're able to think outside the box and create visions that go beyond conventional wisdom.

► **Opportunity Excavator:** You start with a visionary idea and begin to refine it by unearthing opportunities in creative places.

► **Innovative Idea Strategist:** You are challenged by solving problems with innovative ideas that lead to forging a new path.

► **Possibility Architect:** You are intellectually fired up by the act of tackling big problems and finding and building solutions that can change the world.

▶ **Strategic Visionary:** You are exceptional at creating a vision and outlining the precise steps needed to achieve that vision.

▶ **Visionary Change Maker:** You are challenged when you are making big changes that are targeted toward helping people, society, or an organization.

Strategist: Creating the Path

▶ **Analytical Solution Strategist:** You are challenged by pulling back the curtain on small and large problems and solving them by learning new concepts and analytics.

▶ **Efficiency Strategist:** You are challenged by reviewing problems from every angle and creating better, more efficient ways to reach the end result.

▶ **People Strategist:** Your innate ability is in the process of connecting with people, getting their buy-in, and delivering what they need through providing the right personnel-related solutions.

▶ **Possibility Strategist:** You are challenged by thinking big and creating something new that has never been thought of before.

▶ **Results Strategist:** You are challenged when presented with an end result to achieve and thrive in creating the process that will ensure a good result is attained consistently.

▶ **Training Results Strategist:** You are challenged by achieving a result through training or teaching others on a process or product.

▶ **Solutions Excavator:** You have a unique and powerful way of unearthing creative solutions.

Synthesize: Bringing People and Ideas Together

▶ **Collaboration Strategist:** You are challenged by bringing people together to solve a problem.

▶ **Diagnostic Problem Solver:** You ask questions to

understand the entire problem or scenario, and you zero in on a clear and actionable solution.

▶ **Discerning Ideator:** You are most challenged when you are dissecting or breaking down problems and then generating lots of creative solutions on how they can be improved upon or moved forward.

▶ **Synthesis Expert:** You are challenged by the process of bringing multiple concepts together to form one hypothesis or solution.

Catalyst: Igniting Opportunity

▶ **Connection Catalyst:** You are challenged by approaching problems via the connections you can create to get things done.

▶ **Holistic Crisis Problem Solver:** You are challenged by solving problems that occur in a crisis. Your balanced ability to see all angles is even more appreciated and needed when times get tough.

▶ **Social Advocate:** You are challenged by thinking through decisions and always considering the

people side of things. You innately think in terms of how everything will impact people.

▶ **Team Maximizer:** You are exceptional at solving team efficiency problems that don't have an obvious solution.

Builders: Ideas and Structures

▶ **Creative Results Architect:** You are totally engaged when you are able to dive into a challenge and engineer an unconventional result to solve a problem.

▶ **Deal Conductor:** You can manage multiple work streams at the same time in rapid formation while working toward a common high-impact result.

▶ **Design Strategist:** You are challenged by devising unique ways to create design. It's in the creative process of design that you thrive.

▶ **Experience Producer:** You are engaged by the process of creating a sensory experience, such as an event (versus a tangible product).

▶ **Innovative Rebuilder:** You are challenged by the

process of taking something apart and rebuilding it into something that works better.

▶ **Language and Idea Architect:** You are challenged when coming up with a new idea that no one has thought of before or putting words together that make something compelling.

▶ **New Business Growth Strategist:** You are driven by thinking about growth and, more specifically, growing a business. It's exciting for you to think of a variety of business growth challenges and come up with solutions.

Using Your Genius at Work

Once you have identified your genius, you'll realize that you have a powerful capability within you just waiting to be exercised. Finding the connection between your genius and your personality allows you to understand the precise work you should be doing as well as the ideal environment for you to operate in. Since I am an Insight Excavator and an extrovert, ideally I am working with people to help them optimize their work performance. I'm happiest when I'm having deep discussions with my clients to uncover patterns within their responses to my questions that allow me to identify insights. This is a starting point for meaningful change in their lives. I wouldn't be as happy or engaged with my work if I wasn't interacting with others on a regular basis.

Understanding your genius and how you can use it will help you describe what you bring to the table during a job interview or performance review. By explaining what you're good at and what you're not good at, you can easily demonstrate how you will add value to the position you're applying for. Knowing your genius is the first step toward guiding a conversation about finding or creating the right job fit for you, not you for it.

Within your current job, you can use your genius to maximize your potential, meet the challenges that you are excited about, and reframe or delegate the ones you aren't. Look at how you're prioritizing your time and the work you're managing. Most of us usually have more work than we can realistically accomplish. Find out if you can prioritize your load and delegate the tasks that don't light you up. **Through prioritizing and delegating, you can spend more time and effort on the work that is aligned with who you are.** You can also get the right support to help meet your obligations.

My client Miranda's genius was a Crisis Problem Solver. She thrived when things went wrong, and she was known as being levelheaded even in the worst of circumstances. Miranda noticed that when she was asked to resolve lots of crises in her office that she was excited. Tracking the frequency with which others asked her to solve their problems also gave her the awareness that she should be spending even more of her time on crisis situations. She started rethinking the portion of her work that wasn't crisis oriented. She started delegating day-to-day set tasks to other people, and she advocated for evolving her role into one that was a better fit for her genius.

Customizing Work for Junior-Level Employees

If you are in an entry-level position or are an individual contributor—meaning you don't manage a team or have a lot of freedom to organize your workload—the process of integrating your genius into your job may look different from that of someone who has more control over their time. If there is no possible way for you to create or find a project or set of tasks that is more aligned with your genius, that may be a sign that your job isn't the right one for you. However, you may have the power to change your role within the company if you are able to identify a problem and a solution, which is exactly where your genius comes in handy. Have a conversation with your manager, and mention the type of work that is a better fit for you. Ask if he or she can help you find opportunities that are better suited for you. Or show your manager how you can provide more value to the company by solving problems outside your current role. You may be surprised at how receptive others are to this kind of approach.

If you're not able to use your genius in your current role as much as you would like but see a potentially better fit within your company, it might be worth it to bide your time and stick it out at your current job until you can get promoted or switch departments. Knowing that you can't fully use your genius now but will in the future is a much better way to operate than not knowing why you feel stuck.

How to Say No

Your manager will assume you're in the right job unless you say otherwise. After all, a manager can't read your mind. It's important to initiate conversations with your manager to discuss potential opportunities to create a better fit between your genius and the work you do every day, sometimes even by turning down projects or assignments that clearly do not align with your genius. You can do this strategically by suggesting alternatives to you owning the project, such as advocating for someone who's a better fit to own it. It's even more persuasive if you can find the person, talk to them about their bandwidth and interest, and then sell the idea together. This is also a great way to increase productivity. The more you can suggest ways to make things more efficient and get better results, the more wins you achieve for you and your organization.

You may be concerned that saying no to a project or task could be risky. Won't your manager think you're slacking off or that you're not a team player? It's possible that they might, and that's why the way you frame the conversation is incredibly important. Be sure to focus the discussion around your desire to do the best possible job at each task and your belief that the company will benefit by using your abilities to the fullest. Have the discussion in person, not over email or Slack, and bring any evidence of past successes you might have to illustrate the points you want to make about your strengths. In the end, even if your manager isn't willing to move the task off your plate, hopefully they will be impressed by the thought you're putting into your performance and will remember the conversation when other assignments come up.

Overall, is there any way to bring more of your genius into this work? For example, you may be able to take a boring or laborious task and create a new process to make it more efficient. Are there ways you can proactively expand your role to include work that is a better fit and will help your team or organization achieve its goals? Be creative, and don't be afraid to push the envelope of possibility. After all, being bold is a leadership trait, so the right company will recognize your efforts, see your high potential, and want to help you be happy, fulfilled, and effective.

What to Do If You Can't Use Your Genius at Work

If you rarely use your genius at work, it's difficult to find ways to use it more frequently, and you don't have a clear sense of when you might advance within the company to a better-fitting role, it's probably time to change jobs. This might be a scary realization, but remember that **putting in the effort to find work that aligns with your genius is a great investment in your future happiness and success.**

The good news is that once you have identified what your genius is, the entire world of work is open to you. Your genius can be applied to almost any industry. This may sound counterintuitive (*if my genius is a Design Strategist, don't I have to work in a design firm?*), but there are infinite ways you can apply your genius to your career. The key is knowing what it is and then being able to speak with authority on its value. For example, if you are a Solution Excavator, you are challenged when you are excavating solutions to complex problems by filtering out what isn't working. You can see through the data and other variables easily to find a clear solution. This genius can be applied to many different problems in a variety of industries, whether it's technology, finance, or something else altogether.

Advocate for who you are, and be proactive about seeking opportunities that are a better fit. Industries and jobs are changing at such a rapid rate that job-specific knowledge is becoming less important. The problems we face at work are always changing, but the need for people who solve problems is only increasing. You just need to be able to speak about the ways you best like to problem solve or how your ideal way of thinking is critical for certain kinds of problems. If you have spent years working in real estate but you have a strong desire to shift to the health industry, show how you solved problems in real estate, and apply that genius to the health industry or to a specific role you're interested in.

A lot of people wait around for the perfect job to land in their lap versus going out and uncovering one or even creating one, either as an entrepreneur or in an organization that will allow them to capitalize on their strengths. Taking initiative, showing how you can

fill a need, and being proactive about finding opportunities will put you far ahead of the majority of other
job seekers.

The Next Step: Moving into the Zone of Genius

Once you understand your genius, you can start to
own how challenged you are with your job. This means
seeing new ways to use your genius, being more productive, and ultimately having more fun at work. By
knowing who you are and what you do best, you can
choose the activities that make you feel more excited
about your job. The next step is to create a Zone of
Genius—a space where you can combine your unique
intellectual ability with your ultimate purpose.

PART 2

Impact

Quit Following Your Passion and Find Your Purpose

How many times have you heard "follow your passion" as a suggestion on how to direct your career? Unfortunately, this well-meaning advice to find work you're passionate about has sent too many people on a frustrating quest to turn a hobby into a career. The problem with following passions is that they are, by definition, fleeting—they burn hard but die fast. Your passions are what bring you joy in the moment, which is why you can have a lot of them. A passion can also be flamed by something new, but once you've figured it out, your enthusiasm wanes. It's important to understand what passions are and how they relate to you as an individual. They don't define who you are or what you are good at. They describe what you like or sometimes love. Passions are also emotional, which means they change. This is incredibly important to know when considering them as career advice. It doesn't work to follow your passion.

Well-intentioned friends and family may dole out career advice based on their observances of your passions. For instance, I have a passion for cooking. I enjoy it because I don't do it that often, and what I love about it is not so much the actual meal planning or creation—it's bringing people together over a meal and the challenge of testing my culinary limits. Plenty of people have come to my dinner parties and said, "Oh my gosh, everything is so delicious! You should open a restaurant."

If I had less awareness of my genius and purpose, I'd seriously consider it, possibly thinking, *Maybe they're right. I should ditch the hard work of running my own business and go to work for someone else as a chef.*

But because I know my genius is an Insight Excavator, where I can see patterns in data, draw insights from those patterns, and turn the insights into action, I would only change careers if the opportunity offered me a way to use my genius every day and was in line with my career vision.

Some lucky people may be able use their passion to lead them to a career path that uses their genius and provides them with the right challenge. A passion can provide direction, but if you can't connect it to your genius, it ultimately won't be enough to find the job that brings you sustainable challenge. For instance, I also love fitness. I work out five days a week. If I had decided to follow my passion for fitness directly to a company within that industry without applying my knowledge of my genius, I could have ended up in a role that was aligned with my passion but not my Insight Excavator genius. In that case, I may have ended up bored and frustrated in a job that I felt *should* be perfect for me but wasn't.

As wonderful as it might sound to find a job you enjoy within an area you're passionate about, I have found that the best fit is a job that involves the method of work you're exceptional at—your genius—combined with another aspect of your life that is perhaps even more meaningful and longer-lasting than your passions—your purpose. Your purpose is the impact you make on others that provides meaning to your life. The difference between passion and purpose is the key. **Passions are great in the short run, but your purpose is infinite, because it's connected to who you are and will bring you deeper fulfillment.**

Your purpose is influenced by your personal history and your core emotional challenge. It is a positive expression of a negative experience (or experiences) that has impacted you at the deepest level. Your core emotional challenge represents a recurring emotional reaction to a variety of events in your life or one major event that changed the course of your life from that point forward. As a result of the profound effect this had on you, you find that helping someone else navigate this same challenge is extremely meaningful. If you can use what you've learned—even on a subconscious level—to help others, you've found your purpose. And because of this connection between your own past hurts and their resolution, your purpose is deeper than getting a job in the restaurant industry because you're passionate about food, or working for Spotify because you love music.

Your purpose will endure and provide endless motivation for you by having an impact on others that is directly linked to it, because your core emotional challenge will always be part of who you are. If you have an impact on something greater than yourself, whether it's another person, the planet, or any other cause, and it is directly connected to your own personal experiences, you will easily find work meaningful even when it is difficult. But when that personal connection is missing, even nonprofit work for the most compelling cause can feel like an obligation rather than pure joy.

The Purpose of Purpose

Discovering your purpose is how you can recognize the specific impact that fulfills you by understanding why you are drawn to it. In fact, knowing the kind of impact that motivates you is a career must. Without it, you are missing an essential ingredient for success.

Adam Grant, a professor at the Wharton School of Business, has researched the connection between personal fulfillment and impact at work and examined what motivates workers in settings that range from call centers and mail-order pharmacies to swimming pool lifeguard squads. In each of these situations, Grant has found that employees who know why their work has a meaningful, positive impact on others are not just happier than those who don't; they are vastly more productive.

In one study published in 2007, Grant surveyed employees at a public university's call center who were asked to phone potential contributors and ask for donations. Grant and a team of researchers

arranged for one group of call center workers to meet with scholarship students who were recipients of the school's fund-raising largesse. It wasn't a long meeting, just a five-minute session where the workers were able to interact with the students who benefited from donations to the university. Over the next month, that little chat made a big difference. The callers who had interacted with the scholarship students spent more than twice as many minutes on the phone with potential donors as callers who hadn't attended the meeting, and they brought in vastly more money, a weekly average of $503.22, up from $185.94. This research demonstrates clearly that knowing the impact of your work affects your motivation and performance.

A second theory on motivation comes from Daniel Pink. In his book *Drive: The Surprising Truth About What Motivates Us*, Pink writes that there's a gap between what science knows and what business does. Science tells us clearly that rewards such as money and benefits don't motivate employees, but businesses disregard the research and continue to use these kinds of rewards in hopes of boosting performance and productivity. Often, those benefits do lure high-quality employees into particular jobs. However, free food, game rooms, and even raises do nothing for the day-to-day motivation needed to enjoy work. This paradox leaves employees feeling confused: why don't they feel more motivated in the midst of receiving so many perks? But there really is no mystery. Perks are nice to have, but they don't help you feel more challenged in your job, nor do they provide the long-lasting fulfillment that purpose-related work does.

Pink found that the real drivers of motivation are the following:

1   **Autonomy:** the desire to direct our own lives.

2   **Mastery:** the urge to get better at something that matters to you (which I believe is linked to genius).

3 **Purpose:** the yearning to participate in the service of something larger than ourselves.

Pink writes:

The first two legs of the...tripod, autonomy and mastery, are essential. But for proper balance we need a third leg—purpose, which provides a context for its two mates. Autonomous people working toward mastery perform at very high levels. But those who do so in the service of some greater objective can achieve even more. The most deeply motivated people—not to mention those who are most productive and satisfied—hitch their desires to a cause larger than themselves.

Purpose is clearly essential for being motivated at work. It seems simple enough; if you understand how your job changes people's lives in a way that is meaningful to you, you are more likely to end up having endless energy for your work.

Genius Action Plan: Identify Your Core Emotional Challenge and Use It to Find Your Purpose

Your core emotional challenge is a formative part of your identity that you may not be conscious of. I discovered the power of the core emotional challenge through my fervent quest to uncover what motivates and excites me about work. Once I understood it, I saw that it was the answer to finding my purpose.

I grew up on a dairy farm near Charlottesville, Virginia, and I always felt different from the rest of my family. I felt like I wasn't in the right place and that my parents and siblings didn't get who I really was. The most obvious difference was that I'm an extrovert, and the rest of my family is mostly introverted. At school, I was teased for being a farm girl and for participating in community theater, which was something I loved to do

and that made me feel alive. I knew I ultimately wanted a life very different from what I experienced during my childhood. I wanted to live in a big city. I wanted to see the world. Yet my family couldn't relate to my dreams and aspirations. I remember telling my dad that I was going to be living in a city, working as an executive, and he laughed and said, "OK, Laura, let's see." His reaction to my dreams always communicated disbelief in my ability to do things differently from how everyone around me was doing them.

Years later, in the early days of building my business, I spent a lot of time tracking my behavior and thinking, *What is my purpose? What is fulfilling to me?* Nothing I came up with seemed to click until one afternoon when I stepped onto a treadmill at the gym. I looked up to the row of TVs, searching for the one that *Oprah* was on, as I always did. The guest that day described an experience that hit me hard. She said that she felt as if nobody understood her, that she was different and struggled to fit in in a variety of environments. As the guest shared her experience, so many instances of my life where I had felt different came back to me. I realized that this woman was going through the experience of not being seen by important people in her life and that I had often felt the same way, *especially* while growing up. Tears rolled down my cheeks. For the first time, I was able to recognize and articulate a profound loss that I had experienced.

I finally understood that not being seen or understood was a core emotional challenge for me. More than that, I could see how that feeling of not being seen had driven so much of my discontent over the years. Interestingly, in the early part of my career, I sought out jobs where I was not being seen, yet they felt comfortable to me. I accepted jobs that weren't aligned with who I was, and as a result, what was expected of me to succeed was misaligned with my authentic self. My managers saw me through the lens of the job I was performing in, but they couldn't see the real me. Through working with my clients, I have seen that people often unconsciously recreate environments that mirror their family dynamics and values because they feel comfortable. That's the experience I had unconsciously been seeking at Google: a company that looked great on paper and made me look like I was successful to society and to my parents. I realized how that feeling of not being seen and being misplaced and not quite right was an environment that I was recreating over and over again. These companies didn't see me for who I was or had the potential to be **because I didn't see it in myself**.

Once I recognized my core emotional challenge, I knew that helping others be seen for who they were was my purpose in life. And, in fact, I was already doing it! I'm always trying to make people feel seen and understood. I do that by asking lots of questions. I'm endlessly curious about people and what motivates them and helping them see how much value they possess by just being who they are.

Most people don't know what their purpose is

because they haven't taken the time to uncover their core emotional challenge, so it's no wonder that they are clueless about the impact they're having on other people, especially their colleagues. My client Robin is constantly telling her office mates what a great job they are doing. She goes above and beyond in acknowledging their contributions to the team. She has been doing this her entire work life, long before we met. But she never realized or thought about the impact her encouraging words made on others until we talked about it. When I pointed out to her that her desire to acknowledge others was connected to her core emotional challenge, she had an *aha* moment. Robin never realized that her supportive behavior was exactly what she had wanted from her mother but never received. What's more, she was supporting her colleagues all the time without even realizing it. By identifying this purpose, she was able to do more of it and use that purpose as an asset. She was also able to begin to do the internal work to acknowledge herself, which allowed her to feel more confident and able to advocate for herself and the promotion she deserved.

Identify Your Core Emotional Challenge

While we've all faced and conquered a variety of challenges and obstacles, I have found that there is almost always one significant recurring challenge or theme that comes up in my clients' lives. The following exercise is meant to uncover your core emotional challenge by looking at patterns from your past. Be prepared to do some digging and deep thinking. Be honest with your answers, and don't worry how it all translates to your purpose. Once you've completed the questions, you will go back and review them to see where ideas about your purpose may emerge.

Part 1: Childhood, Ages 5–18

1 What was the best part of your childhood from ages five to eighteen? What was the most challenging part? Why?

2 What was the best part of your high school days? What was the most challenging part? Why?

3 How would you describe your home life and your parents' relationship? Was your home life stable?

4 What was the specific impact of your family on you?

5 How did your parents relate to you during this time in your life? Did they support your strengths? Did they have a preconceived idea of what you should do for a career or how you should live your life?

6 How did you reconcile their wishes with your own?

Or if they didn't have any specific wishes, how did their value system or their ideas of success affect your own views of your potential and career choices?

Part 2: College and Adult Life

1 What are some of the emotional challenges that you've experienced during these years?

2 Have you had any experiences or significant emotional challenges in your adult life that have changed you substantially?

3 What are some instances where you've had an extreme emotional reaction to something that others may see as benign? What was the root cause of your negative emotion? These moments are often your core emotional challenge at work.

REFLECTION

Analyze your answers as if you were reading someone else's biography. Write down the most obvious emotional challenges from each time period.

Are you currently facing any of the challenges you listed on the previous page?

Once you've figured out your core emotional challenge or even if you still haven't, review when you are most fulfilled at work. List the moments in the past month when you felt fulfilled by the impact you had. Write down the specific impact you had on other people through your work. Keep in mind that it's easy to generalize with these questions, but I want you to be as specific as possible. For example, if you had a meeting with someone and they said, "Wow, you really helped me," you know you helped them, but in what specific way? It could be that you helped them build their confidence or helped them see themselves in a new light. This is how specific you need to be with this exercise.

Name Your Purpose

Just like naming your genius, it's important to label your core emotional challenge and then create a phrase for your purpose. Mine is *helping others see themselves for who they are.* This phrase grounds me in the impact that is most meaningful to me and allows me to easily see if I am having the impact regularly that is in line with my calling. Here are some phrases that you can use to help you get clear on what yours is:

▶ **Acceptance: Making others feel accepted.** You're fulfilled by being nonjudgmental and receptive to others because you weren't accepted by your family for being who you are.

▶ **Being Heard: Helping others find their voice.** This purpose might stem from growing up in a family where there was little to no communication or feeling like you were never heard. Helping others be open, find their voice, or fine-tune a message they need to share is endlessly fulfilling to you.

▶ **Belonging: Helping people find a place where they belong.** You're motivated by helping people find the exact role in their workplace or life in which they will shine. This likely stems from feeling like you were constantly trying to identify your own place in the world.

▶ **Boldness: Helping others be themselves.** Based on a pattern of hiding yourself because you feared rejection, you want to help others be bold in a way that feels right for them.

▶ **Calmness: Helping others navigate chaos.** If you had to navigate ongoing chaos throughout your childhood, you likely learned a unique skill of adaptation and being calm in the face of a storm. You're fulfilled by helping others navigate a hectic, fast-paced, or disorganized workplace by being a voice of calm and reason.

▶ **Control: Helping others feel in control.** If you felt inadequate and out of control in your early years due to an unstable home life or other events, it's likely

that helping others feel like they can take the reins in their own life is particularly meaningful to you.

▶ **Difference: Helping others follow a different path rather than the expected one.** If you've always been drawn to do something different than what others expected of you but were discouraged from pursuing those things, helping others take the road less traveled will be meaningful for you.

▶ **Failure: Helping others overcome mistakes.** This purpose comes from dealing with the failures of others, most likely your parents or significant others. As a result, you've learned to make good decisions and avoid epic failures that negatively affect others.

▶ **Fairness: Promoting justice.** If you felt unfairly disadvantaged or didn't get the same opportunities as others, it probably stuck with you. As a result, being impartial and advocating for fair treatment of others is not only meaningful to you, but also fundamental to how you operate and help others.

▶ **Freedom: Helping others feel liberated.** If you

ever felt restricted in an unhealthy way, it's motivating to you to help someone else feel free, unencumbered, and able to thrive as they wish.

► **Ideal Environments: Creating spaces that allows people to thrive.** This purpose is rooted in being raised in an environment, especially at school or at home, that felt like the wrong fit. As a result, you love creating ideal environments for others to thrive in.

► **Included: Making others feel included.** You enjoy helping others feel included, because you often felt left out and isolated from others frequently in the past.

► **Opportunities: Opening up options for others.** If your grew up with a lack of opportunities (financial or otherwise), creating them for others offers great fulfillment.

► **Possibility: Helping others step outside of their comfort zone and realize what they're capable of.** Any activity that allows you help others step into possibility is rewarding. This is because you may have felt trapped or grew up in an environment that lacked possibility.

▶ **Potential: Helping others operate at their highest potential.** If you never experienced having someone else help you see or maximize your potential, it's meaningful for you to do this for others.

▶ **Positivity: Being a force of optimism.** If you were raised in an environment that was often critical and negative, you're fulfilled by bringing positivity to as many situations as possible.

▶ **Focus: Helping people realize that their wants and needs matter.** You're motivated by helping others understand that their wants and needs should be a focus because you know the pain of not having your needs be a focus from others.

▶ **Standing Out: Helping others not feel invisible.** You live to help individuals or organizations stand out. You know what it's like to feel invisible, so you strive to help others speak up and say what's on their mind.

▶ **Support: Exceeding expectations by supporting others.** You love supporting others to exceed expectations. You may be counteracting a childhood experience during which the bar for achievement was high and support wasn't provided for you to reach it.

▶ **Understanding: Helping others feel understood despite being different.** This is meaningful for you because being understood by your family and close friends was a constant challenge.

▶ **Value: Making others feeling valued.** If you were raised in a family where who you are was not valued, you may have been encouraged to be someone that you weren't. You therefore want to help others feel valued for being exactly who they are.

▶ **Seen: Helping others see themselves for who they are.** Helping others be seen for who they are is meaningful because you grew up with the struggle of not being seen and understood.

Resolving Your Core Emotional Challenge

For most of my clients, understanding their core emotional challenge allows them to identify blind spots in their behavior. Being able to work on these blind spots can be game-changing in becoming a more powerful leader. Once I recognized my core emotional challenge, I realized that I needed to address my own negative behavior that occurred when I wasn't feeling seen. This meant being more aware of when it happened and addressing the angst it caused within me. It's never possible to completely erase a core emotional challenge from your life, but having a greater awareness of it can be the first step to healing.

The process of working through many different core emotional challenges can vary. However, the work always begins with identifying your core emotional challenge and then giving to yourself what it has taken away.

Once you identify your core emotional challenge,

you may be amazed by how often you notice it surfacing through uncomfortable moments in your work and life. These are the times when you may say to yourself, *Wow, I have no idea why I am in tears over the fact that my friend just canceled our plans last minute.* While the canceled event may have been meaningless, the fact that you feel ignored could be your core emotional challenge, and a small, seemingly benign event in the present can trigger deep-seated pain from the past. Recognizing my core emotional challenge was liberating: when small events occur and cause me to feel unseen, I can step back and say to myself, *Oh wait, this is a core emotional wound. This is bringing me back to a painful event from my past. My reaction right now is a more extreme reaction than what this situation calls for.*

As you begin to notice when your triggers occur, you can begin to modify your reaction to them. According to psychologist John Cacioppo, our brains are wired to pick up more negative information than positive. In fact, our brains take in two-thirds negative

and one-third positive information. This is why our general state of awareness is highly critical. However, we can compensate for this tendency by adding more positive data to any situation. I have found that creating positive mantras that address the negative chatter in our minds when we are triggered by a core emotional challenge can be a highly effective way to move forward and heal. For example, if my negative message is *I'm not being seen*, when I flip the narrative and tell myself that I'm in fact being seen, it calms me down. Sometimes, I just need to say *I see myself. I'm valuable.*

Rewire Negative Mental Chatter

You can work to reduce the power that your core emotional challenge has over you by rewiring your brain and replacing negative thought patterns with positive ones. To rewire negative mental chatter, you first have to notice the specific messages that are manifesting in your mind. Once you do this, you can create new, more positive messages to replace the negative ones. By doing so, you literally create new neural pathways in your brain that connect to the thoughts of the present instead of memories from the past. For example, if your negative chatter is telling you how unsuccessful and worthless you are, reverse this message to *I am a worthwhile person with a genius that is highly valuable, and as a result, I will be very successful.*

As you repeat this positive statement, you should experience two benefits: you immediately feel better, and you will feel more confident over time. You will see evidence that this new statement is true because you'll be more inclined to notice the aspects of your life that match the positive messages you're creating. What we think becomes a reality, which is why when you are overcome by your negative chatter, life can seem grim.

The Next Step

Now that you know your core emotional challenge, you know what your purpose is and are ready to put it into action. In the next chapter, you will learn how to use your purpose to create more fulfillment at work, and you'll see just how often you're having an impact on others that is meaningful to you.

chapter 4

Fulfillment = Impact

When I worked for Capital One, my colleagues and I would say regularly, "It's not like we're saving lives." This was how we articulated the lack of personal connection we felt to the impact of our work. It wasn't clear how what I did day to day affected people other than allowing them to have a credit card. I was in my twenties, I was achievement driven, and finding fulfillment through my work didn't seem like a realistic goal, nor was it a priority.

This is not to say that a credit card company doesn't have an impact. Giving someone a financial product that allows them to make purchasing decisions can be empowering—it just wasn't something I related to on a deeply personal level. Now, I know that the problem wasn't me or my job. I was just a poor fit because the impact the job had wasn't impactful to me: there was no connection to my purpose. Not everyone can save lives, but **everyone deserves to feel that their work is contributing to something that's meaningful to them**. In fact, it's crucial in order to reach the highest levels of success. If I had known then what I know now, I could have figured out a way to be more strategic with my genius and my purpose and sought out a job within the organization that was a better fit.

Intrinsic Motivation versus Extrinsic Motivation

Intrinsic motivation refers to when you engage in an activity because it is rewarding in and of itself. At work, examples include the following:

▶ Volunteering to run a project because the work is aligned with your genius

- ▶ Creating a PowerPoint to help your colleagues understand a difficult concept that interests you
- ▶ Going for a promotion because the work excites you

In contrast, *extrinsic motivation* occurs when you are motivated to engage in an activity for the sole reason of earning a reward or avoiding punishment. At work, examples include:

- ▶ Completing a project to please your manager
- ▶ Working hard to close a deal in time to receive a bonus
- ▶ Going for a promotion just for the raise

When I was working at Google, I suffered from a complete lack of intrinsic motivation. I was always trying to prove my worth, both to my manager and myself. When you don't feel motivated by the work you're doing, you have to cultivate your motivation using willpower, which is, unfortunately, the most common way people are motivated at work today. You know you are operating under these conditions when you have to push yourself to finish a project that requires you to do something that you're not good at, present to your team a vision that you don't feel excited to create, or do detailed work that feels excruciatingly not right for you. This pattern causes stress and anxiety and the all-too-common burnout.

Some people say that this is just the way work is: you aren't supposed to jump for joy over projects you manage, and it's OK that work feels like, well, work. If someone says that to you, you must recognize that that is a belief system that they've decided to adopt. Believing that work should feel like work is a choice. Oftentimes this choice is not conscious, but times are changing. In fact, most people, given the conscious choice, want to have work that they enjoy and that provides meaning. This is particularly true for millennials and Gen Z, who now make up the majority of our workforce. According to Enso's World Value Index, 68 percent of millennials say creating change in the world is a personal goal that they actively pursue. Millennials are also known to choose experiences over material goods, so it's no surprise that they are more focused on purpose and impact than profits. According to an article by Kiely Kuligowski on Business News Daily, Gen Z, now entering the workforce, are even more focused on having meaning, connection, autonomy, and flexibility. They are also more inclusive and welcoming of diversity. The younger generations are driving shifts in how the business world operates, and knowing this information not only makes you a better manager to younger people but also allows you to explore something that every human desires and deserves: work they're good at and that brings meaning.

Purpose and impact are the fuel that keeps you going. They are what gets you up in the morning and your access to endless motivation and endless energy for the work you're doing. Just as Adam Grant has proven, if you know your impact, your performance will improve. Knowing the impact that is meaningful for you will not only improve performance but also connect you to your purpose.

Measure Your Impact by Assessing How Often You're Using Your Purpose

Once you're clear on what your purpose is and how you want to impact others, you can begin to assess how you can apply that to your work life.

Step One: Determine if your purpose is aligned with your company, your organization, or your own business. One way to figure that out is by looking at its mission and values statement. How does it express or communicate the impact the company wants to have on its customers?

Step Two: See if you can align your purpose to your company's mission statement. If so, it's likely there is some aspect of the business that will provide intrinsic motivation for you. If you are interviewing with a new

company, determine whether its daily actions reflect this mission statement by asking specific questions of the person you're interviewing with. For example, you can ask them to share behavioral indications that the values and mission are honored on a regular basis. Unfortunately, lots of companies promote mission and values statements that are little more than window dressing. You'll want to make sure that any company you work for is actually being who they say they are.

Maximize Your Impact

Knowing the relationship between your purpose and the impact you make will provide you with the intrinsic motivation you are looking for. When you have endless motivation for your work, you will have the energy to achieve at a level you didn't think possible. Yet so many people still see purpose as a nice-to-have and not an essential aspect of their work life.

You can gauge your impact by taking a close look at who you work with. Depending on your job, those people might be your coworkers, your direct reports (if you are a manager), or your customers. Do you have a consistent type of impact that makes a positive change to the company? Are the people around you developing or growing in a way that feels meaningful to you because of your help?

It's amazing how unaware we can sometimes be of our effect on others. I once had a friend who didn't realize until he left the company how powerful his impact was. His purpose was helping people work effectively through conflicts. This work was extremely meaningful to him, and he helped people in this way all the time. He had always made a point of ensuring that everyone on his team was working effectively, and he was often tapped to help resolve conflicts within other teams. It was obvious to everyone that he made a positive impact on others, but how much he had made a difference to the organization didn't register with him. When he left the company to start his own business, he received dozens of emails from colleagues who all shared how much they enjoyed working with him and how strongly they felt his impact. In that moment, he felt overwhelmed with a feeling of purpose. Imagine if he had recognized his impact sooner—he could have had that feeling of fulfillment every day. This is the importance of identifying your purpose and then making sure it's being leveraged as a tangible impact all the time.

Entering Your Zone of Genius: Combining Genius and Impact

Getting into your Zone of Genius is possible for everyone, and I promise it makes work exhilarating. In the ideal scenario, you actively use your genius and feel the impact of your purpose at work. It's like putting together a puzzle. You need to strategically create the work that will allow you to use your genius and then monitor the impact to confirm that you're fulfilling your purpose. The two go hand in hand more often than you realize, meaning that the way you create an impact on others that is most meaningful is by engaging your genius in that process. For example, when I help people feel seen and understand themselves, I am doing that by using my Insight Excavator genius. It's in these moments that I am actively in my Zone of Genius.

I like to describe it this way: **you're in your Zone of Genius when you're using both your head and your heart**. Your genius stems from the intellectual challenge and brainpower necessary to do the work, and your purpose drives the impact that fills your soul. When you're working within your Zone of Genius, you feel both challenged and fulfilled. You're making an impact that's meaningful to you, and even more powerfully, you feel that your work is your calling. When my clients are in their Zone of Genius, they describe it as feeling unstoppable. They also reach their career visions faster than they expected. They stop feeling drained by work, they are energized and excited about what they are doing, and they

constantly create new and even more exciting opportunities to tackle.

Working within your Zone of Genius 100 percent of the time isn't realistic, but you can aim to use it often in your day-to-day life if you're conscious and proactive about it. Using the Zone of Genius tracker is a great way to tell if you are actively creating opportunities that are right for you and, if not, provide the insight for you to correct your course quickly. You can download a copy of the Zone of Genius tracker and a Word document that has all the above exercises in a user-friendly format at lauragarnett.com/thegeniushabit.

I strive to ensure that 70 percent of my workweek is spent doing work that is aligned with my Zone of Genius. The other 30 percent is work that I know I *have* to do; I know that it doesn't challenge me intellectually or have the impact that fulfills me, but it needs to get done so I can continue with the work that does.

Common Roadblocks to Operating in Your Zone of Genius

Once you're clear about what your Zone of Genius is and you're actively working to ensure you're using it, there will inevitably be roadblocks. Here are a few to look out for.

You easily lose sight of yourself and lose confidence in the face of conflict with others.

This one is subtle but prolific. It means that when someone you work with says or does something that makes you feel like your opinions, thoughts, or ideas aren't valuable, you shrink. You think they're right, and you slowly start to think that who you are isn't needed or valuable. Over time, your confidence diminishes, and you lose sight of who you are, all while trying to prove your worth by being someone you're not. In these situations, you need to do the reverse. First, give feedback when this happens. If you're not working in a company that values feedback, then take note, because feedback is important. If you never receive any, it's a sign that your organization isn't a high-performance culture. Second, do the internal work to tell yourself that you're valuable even when you fail or aren't contributing in a way that is needed for that moment. Remind yourself that your Zone of Genius is valuable, but maybe it's not valuable in this moment or potentially in this job or organization. When you're clear about who you are, you don't question your value, and you can more easily see this type of scenario as an indication of a job misfit or a one-off problem that can be solved with feedback, meaning it was most likely unintentional. Take action, and do not lose yourself.

You're too busy to focus on being in the zone.

This is probably the most common roadblock. Everybody is busy, and the busyness is not going away. Taking the time to know your Zone of Genius

and operate in it requires awareness and attention. In many ways, it adds another hygiene habit to your work life. I get it; it's not easy to add things to an already busy day and life. However, doing it will make you more productive. It's kind of like the idea that if you take the time to work out, you will be more energized to accomplish more with the time you have. Operating in your Zone of Genius is the same. If you are in the zone, your productivity doubles. It's your decision, but

I couldn't imagine not paying attention to something that ensures excitement, joy, and fulfillment at work, along with long-term guaranteed success.

Your well-being takes a dive, and you don't have the energy to do the work.

Nobody is perfect, and when sickness or health issues come up, everything else goes out the window. That's understandable. This is a way of operating that is meant to amp up your performance, so if you're not performing, give yourself a break. Prioritizing your well-being is nonnegotiable, and your Zone of Genius is a great partner to that. When you feel great, you're healthy, and you just worked out, operating in your Zone of Genius takes you to the next level on top of that good feeling. Well-being is an essential partner to operating in your Zone of Genius.

You lose hope in the face of big failures and disappointments.

Failures are inevitable. It's how you manage them that sets successful people apart from those who aren't. Look at failures as opportunities to learn and grow. They shouldn't deter you from being in your Zone of Genius, and they will help you learn how to be more effective along the way. I talk a lot about the value of failures in *The Genius Habit*. Reading that is a great next step after you've mastered being in the zone. Just remember, failures don't mean you're a failure; they mean that you're stretching your comfort zone and are, in fact, becoming more successful. Don't let them deter you.

You get distracted by external rewards.

This is a really common one. It is also dangerously subtle. You feel like you're making progress, and then you're offered a huge bonus or a raise to stay in a job that you've decided isn't right for you. Or you're told

you're doing a great job and you're highly valued, even though you know you're not doing the work that is really right for you; you're just a hard worker and are on the brink of burnout. Or you're interviewing for the next opportunity, you're clear about what you want, and you get an offer that is financially beyond what you could imagine, doing work that you know isn't right for you. We've been taught that these rewards are more important than enjoying our jobs. It's easy to be seduced by them, because in that moment, your brain looks into the future and imagines how happy you will be with the security and the money, but it doesn't predict the boredom, frustration, or unhappiness that come from work that isn't aligned with who you are. This one requires you to resist the societal conditioning that has been programmed into you. This is where knowing your Zone of Genius can be game-changing. It can help you see through the rewards. If a job won't allow you to do the thinking or problem solving that you're best at and have an impact that is meaningful, just say no. Walk away, and trust that when you say no, it opens the door of opportunity for the right job to come through.

If you can resist these common roadblocks and increase your awareness of when you are operating in your Zone of Genius and when you're not, you will experience a different world of work. This is a world that I believe we all want and deserve to have. This is a world that I have had clients enter and never want to leave. It feels like you've won the lottery.

The average American will spend ninety thousand hours working in their career, more for us younger generations that will most likely not retire at sixty-five. Don't you want to make the most of those ninety thousand hours? I know I do. I know you do too. Welcome to a process that has not only supercharged the trajectory of my success but has turned my career journey into one of the greatest joys of my life. Good luck!

AFTERWORD

When I was at my lowest point, I'll never forget the thoughts that were swirling through my head. *What if I am not able to create something meaningful with my career? I feel like I have something special to bring to the world, but what is it? What am I best at? What is the impact in the world that will fulfill me?*

The powerlessness I felt was overwhelming. I had little support, and I couldn't seem to find the answers I was seeking. There were hundreds of books that talked about how to create success, but I couldn't find anything that spoke to how I could tap into my own gifts and then use them in a powerful way.

My hope is that by reading this book, you never

again have to feel the way I did. Once you begin the process of knowing your Zone of Genius, those thoughts will disappear.

In the end, this book is meant to teach you more about you. What has been so fascinating to me in my eleven years of working with this material is that very few people are in touch with their greatest strengths. Seldom are they wielding the power that is readily available within themselves. That power increases when you know your Zone of Genius.

If you do the work that is outlined in this book, I promise it will change how you feel about yourself and your career.

I hope you will also experience more joy. Tapping into your genius and purpose at work is like nothing you've experienced before. There is a relaxation that comes with this realization, which builds confidence about your career, and that confidence is magnetizing. You'll inspire others just by being who you are and doing the work you were meant to do.

My dream is that everyone will do the work to become an inspiration not only to themselves but also to those around them. When joy, not drudgery, is associated with work, our society will be different. Living up to your true potential is the greatest gift you can give yourself and the world.

→ ACKNOWLEDGMENTS

This book started its inception seven months after the launch of *The Genius Habit*. Interestingly, in the aftermath of *The Genius Habit*, I had requests for smaller versions, something that could be read in less than an hour to get a sense of my work. Here it is. What I see this book being is an appetizer to the concept of *The Genius Habit*. If you read this and love it, go ahead and go for the main course with *The Genius Habit*. On its own, though, *Find Your Zone of Genius* is something that everyone should be focused on. It's a framework for knowing who you are and showing up as such on a daily basis. It's the first and most critical step toward having the success and joy you want at work. What has been so fun is seeing my daughter's personality emerge throughout the book writing process. I see signs of her genius peeking through, and nothing is more delightful than knowing that it's my job to help her value herself and see her genius as one of the most valuable assets in her life. My wish is that we all can give this to each other. Be who you are, value it, and bring it forth to the world.

As with any book, it's a reflection of a team of amazing people.

My Book Team

My agent, Myrsini: from the moment we met, it was always meant to be. You have been one of the most joyous parts of this journey, and I love working with you. The ability to see potential and cultivate it is certainly your genius.

Anna, Meg, and Bridget, my editors. Working with each of you has been a peak working experience. Your speed, thoroughness, and ability to really "get" the work has been a godsend. This project would not be what it is without both of you.

Thank you to Sourcebooks and everyone there for being an ideal publisher. From welcoming me with open arms and rolling out the red carpet when I visited, to diving in and giving me endless support for the entire book process to going above and beyond with marketing projects to support the launch of the book, I could not have asked for a better partner in bringing this book to the world.

Liz, your genius shines through with your marketing excellence. Thanks for the support, ideas, and assistance in getting this book out in the world in a meaningful way.

Miranda, Adrian, Abby, Erika, and Lisa: thank you all for your continual support and help. You are my dream team! I love working with you all and couldn't do what I do without you. You all have been instrumental in this second book-writing process.

My Support Circle

To James, my partner, and my daughter, Zoe. You two are the lights of my life and continue to inspire me with everything you both do.

Special thanks again to Jenny Blake, Cybele Loening, and Teri Geotz. Your support and availability for ideas and feedback for this book were essential!

Mom and Dad, thank you always for giving me life and so much more, but most importantly for my ambition, my discipline, and my high bar for excellence. This second book wouldn't be here today without those essential qualities I learned from you both.

To my niece and nephews, Ella, Beck, and Connor, you are the future generation of our family, and your enthusiasm for life inspires me. I can see your Zones of Genius emerging and the tremendous value that you have to offer the world. I can't wait to witness your greatness in whatever form it takes.

ABOUT THE AUTHOR

Photo by Alyssa Peek

LAURA GARNETT is a performance strategist, TEDx speaker, mother, and author of *The Genius Habit*. She works with hundreds of CEOs and executives to identify their Zone of Genius™ and leverage it in their day-to-day work. She has brought her expertise to more than forty companies, including OpenTable, Google, LinkedIn, and Geometry Global. Prior to launching her company, Garnett Consulting, she honed her marketing, branding, and career-refining skills at Capital One, American Express, IAC, and Google.

Note from the Author

At the time that we were putting the finishing touches on this book, the COVID-19 pandemic hit. During such a crisis, there is a lot of uncertainty about how our lives, the economy, and the world will shift as a result. One thing, however, remains constant, and that is who you are and the value you offer to the world. My hope has always been that everyone can find their Zone of Genius and own it. As a result of this crisis and its economic consequences, it's not just my hope, it's actually essential that you know and own your value. I wish you the best as you make the most of these uncertain times

Stay Connected

Sign up for my free biweekly *The Zone* newsletter at lauragarnett.com, where I offer free advice, access to my recently published articles on *Forbes* and *Business Insider*, and more. I also share my own personal journey as it's happening as well as discuss new evolutions of my work and focus.

You can also follow me on Instagram @laura garnett1 for inspiring quotes and ongoing performance building suggestions.

Go Deeper

Work directly with me: My genius is at its best when working with individuals one-on-one or with executive teams. I have a variety of individual and team packages. Visit lauragarnett.com/services to review how I can help you or your executive team take your work and team performance to new heights.

Purchase *The Genius Habit* Book Club (lauragarnett .com/bookclub): Want to take the lead and help your work team learn your Zones of Genius and take your performance to the next level? Check out the book club, where you will find videos, agendas, and guidelines on how to run an effective book club experience with *The Genius Habit*.

Work with me privately or with a Zone of Genius coach: I have sought out and trained some of the best coaches I can find on the Genius Habit approach. If you are interested in learning more, please go to lauragarnett.com/services.

Have me be a select executive coach for your organization: I thrive when working with companies that are committed to their people and are supportive of them maximizing their potential. Visit lauragarnett.com/contact to reach out. It would be great to explore the opportunity to work with your leaders.

Speaking and workshops: I would love to come speak to your company or at your event. *The Genius Habit* talk or workshop is ideal for team off-site training, annual sales meetings, or any event that is focused on success or work performance. Please go to lauragarnett.com/speaking for more information.

NEW! Only from Simple Truths®

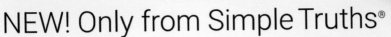

IGNITE READS
spark impact in just one hour

IGNITE READS IS A NEW SERIES OF 1-HOUR READS WRITTEN BY WORLD-RENOWNED EXPERTS!

These captivating books will help you become the best version of yourself, allowing for new opportunities in your personal and professional life. Accelerate your career and expand your knowledge with these powerful books written on today's hottest ideas.

TRENDING BUSINESS AND PERSONAL GROWTH TOPICS

Read in an hour or less

Leading experts and authors

Bold design and captivating content